T5-COD-863

BEST Travel Activity Book EVER

word finds
mazes
coloring pages
sketch starters
fun facts
inspiring devotions
and much more

BroadStreet KIDS

BroadStreet Kids
Savage, Minnesota, USA

BroadStreet Kids is an imprint of BroadStreet Publishing Group, LLC.
Broadstreetpublishing.com

Best Travel Activity Book Ever

© 2019 by BroadStreet Publishing®

978-1-4245-5907-7

All rights reserved. No part of this publication may be reproduced, distributed, or transmitted in any form or by any means, including photocopying, recording, or other electronic or mechanical methods, without the prior written permission of the publisher, except in the case of brief quotations embodied in critical reviews and certain other noncommercial uses permitted by copyright law.

Scripture quotations marked (NLT) are taken from the Holy Bible, New Living Translation, copyright © 1996, 2004, 2007. Used by permission of Tyndale House Publishers, Inc., Carol Stream, Illinois 60188. All rights reserved. Scripture quotations marked (NIV) are taken from the Holy Bible, New International Version®, niv®. Copyright © 1973, 1978, 1984, 2011 by Biblica, Inc.™ Used by permission of Zondervan. All rights reserved worldwide. www.zondervan.com. The "NIV" and "New International Version" are trademarks registered in the United States Patent and Trademark Office by Biblica, Inc.™ Scripture quotations marked (NCV) are taken from the New Century Version®. Copyright © 2005 by Thomas Nelson. Used by permission. All rights reserved. Scripture quotations marked (ESV) are from the ESV® Bible (The Holy Bible, English Standard Version®), copyright © 2001 by Crossway, a publishing ministry of Good News Publishers. Used by permission. All rights reserved. Scripture quotations marked (TLB) are taken from The Living Bible copyright © 1971. Used by permission of Tyndale House Publishers, Inc., Carol Stream, Illinois 60188. All rights reserved. Scripture quotations marked (ICB) are taken from the International Children's Bible®. Copyright © 1986, 1988, 1999 by Thomas Nelson. Used by permission. All rights reserved. Scripture quotations marked (NIRV) are taken from the Holy Bible, New International Reader's Version®, NIrV® Copyright © 1995, 1996, 1998, 2014 by Biblica, Inc.™ Used by permission of Zondervan. All rights reserved worldwide. www.zondervan.com. The "NIrV" and "New International Reader's Version" are trademarks registered in the United States Patent and Trademark Office by Biblica, Inc.™

Design by Chris Garborg | garborgdesign.com
Created, edited, and compiled by Michelle Winger | literallyprecise.com
Mazes licensed from mazegenerator.net.

Printed in the United States.

19 20 21 22 23 24 25 7 6 5 4 3 2

Introduction

Whether you're in the car, on a plane, at a campsite, or lying on the beach, grab some pencils and exercise your brain with this activity book. Inspiring themes will help develop both your relationship with God and your personal character, making you a better travel companion.

Each of the twelve themes has a devotion, prayer, travel highlight, fun facts, and challenging activities that are designed to keep you focused on topics that encourage you both close to home and far away. Use your mind to solve puzzles and your imagination to create. Spend time in prayer, asking God to help you put these themes into practice daily.

Enjoy this unique activity book where you can have fun and be inspired at the same time!

CHANGE

Whatever is good and perfect is a gift coming down to us from God our Father, who created all the lights in the heavens. He never changes.

JAMES 1:17 NLT

When people talk about the person they trust the most, they sometimes describe that person as their rock. That's because rocks are dependable. They don't run away, they don't hide, they don't become flowers or snakes, and they aren't easily broken. We also say that God is our rock. He is steady, he is strong, and he doesn't change.

When we travel to different places, we might experience many changes. The time of day, food, weather, or landscape could be very different than what we are used to. Sometimes that makes us feel uncomfortable. We might get nervous or even become afraid.

God never changes, and he never stops watching over you. He created all the amazing places you will ever travel to, and he knows right where you are at every moment! Trust God to be your rock as you travel and enjoy experiencing things that are different than what you are used to.

Use the alphabet code to unlock the secret message.

◎	⅄	☼	□	💧	✓	❖	♦	✿	✞	☺	✎	≈
A	B	C	D	E	F	G	H	I	J	K	L	M

★	↑	↓	●	⌘	☸	✖	⁂	▣	✸	✂	※	❄
N	O	P	Q	R	S	T	U	V	W	X	Y	Z

✞ 💧 ☸ ⁂ ☸ ☼ ♦ ⌘ ✿ ☸ ✖

_ _ _ _ _ _ _ _ _ _ _

✿ ☸ ✖ ♦ 💧 ☸ ◎ ≈ 💧

_ _ _ _ _ _ _ _ _

※ 💧 ☸ ✖ 💧 ⌘ □ ◎ ※

_ _ _ _ _ _ _ _ _

◎ ★ □ ✖ ↑ □ ◎ ※

_ _ _ _ _ _ _ _

Answer on page 124

Dear God, change can be scary, like moving to a new house or going to a new school. But I also know that changes can be good for me. Help me to trust you when things are changing because I know you want what is best for me. Thank you that you never change; you are always with me.

Change one letter at a time to turn ROCK into HOPE.

ROCK

_ _ _ _ framework for holding a shelf

_ _ _ _ contest of speed

_ _ _ _ starchy seeds

_ _ _ _ ready for eating

_ _ _ _ a strong cord

HOPE

Answer on page 124

Unscramble the letters to read the message.

E W   V E A H   H I T S

_ _   _ _ _ _   _ _ _ _

O P E H   S A   N A

_ _ _ _   _ _   _ _

C H A R O N   O R F   H E T

_ _ _ _ _ _   _ _ _   _ _ _

L O U S   F R I M   N A D

_ _ _ _   _ _ _ _   _ _ _

C R E U S E

_ _ _ _ _ _ .

Answer on page 124

Find the Different animals who Change in their surroundings.

G

C U R

A N U R H

T X H E V Z S

E X O D S Z Y Z I

R B S N V E I Y I M F

P T U A P A C Q F F R G E

I J W M N N Z J W E R B M Q L

L V H A V F H P S N L T E U S Y T

L P S L P K Q W T Y O T R J F Z R B T

A R B A O L A I B T O E E N J D F R S G U

R U R S Q U M F I Z I O L E M F X V U E P F C

I L J R C R T K F O C L V E B H D A G L P L Q A W

N S R E V V X X V V R V V C M F I I R W E P M G O P M

Q S R G E B B D G X K Y M R S A S K E C G L H M F U D Z J

W H U I A L I L A M O X F G V X H I E T T T O S I V Z H G O A

P T T T Z Z O J D H R T T Z B C O I U I Q P C V Q P P I S

V V R M N A F L A T F I S H H T D Q C R D D O H U W C

D Z I T P A R V W Q E Z I R R O U F S A K Q S J O

M T U V V B E M G W E T D O C C O V T I T C P

I X Q E B W D J H H R B T T X X I C I U S

M M S B I S N T M V T X V U F R C A O

I N A K B E U Z E B R O S C K F W

C O E O T W O E H A R C I N L

O T S I J N L R C B N A B

C H B M X Z F Y S D V

T K G L F N E L U

O J K G C Q D

P K T T D

U X R

S

WORD LIST

ARCTIC FOX	FLOUNDER	STICK INSECT
CATERPILLAR	MIMIC OCTOPUS	TADPOLE
CHAMELEON	PUFFERFISH	TIGER SALAMANDER
CUTTLEFISH	SCOPS OWL	TORTOISE BEETLE
FLATFISH	SEA SQUIRT	TREE FROG

Find your way through the maze!

What Should I Pack?

Tangles aren't good
and I'm in a rush.
What could I use?
Of course, it's my

____

Brush, brush, brush,
without me, it's a waste.
Put me on the bristles.
I am

____

Race to the finish line,
without these you would lose.
Quick tie me up!
I'm your

__________ __________

When it is hot
this is fit for a queen.
To stay away from burns,
put on the

____

Answer on page 124

HIGHLIGHT

HIKING!

Hiking is what we call traveling on foot in the mountains or countryside.

•

You should never hike alone!

•

When you hike without a trail, it's called bushwhacking.

•

One of the earliest recorded hiking expeditions was on the snow mountain Titus in 1744.

•

Hiking is good for your health. It improves your physical, mental, and spiritual wellbeing.

•

The Pacific Crest Trail is 2,650 miles long and usually takes about five months to hike.

List five people who you consider to be your "rocks."

1 ______________________________

2 ______________________________

3 ______________________________

4 ______________________________

5 ______________________________

GUIDANCE

From a place far away I call out to you.
I call out as my heart gets weaker.
Lead me to the safety of a rock
that is high above me.

PSALM 61:2 NIRV

How do you like navigating through a paper maze? Have you ever been in a real maze? Sometimes you get stuck: you hit a dead end or go around in circles. Life can feel a little bit like that in certain moments—you might feel lost or stuck.

The amazing thing about God is that he always knows where you are! You just need to call out to him and ask for help. He can tell you the way to go. Soon enough, you will be headed in the right direction again.

There is nowhere on earth we can go without God knowing we are there. That should be a huge comfort to us in the moments we feel lost.

Which two Pictures are exactly the same?

Answer on page 124

Draw a line from the beginning to the end that passes through each box with a compass in it once. The line can go up, down, left, or right, but cannot go diagonal.

Start here

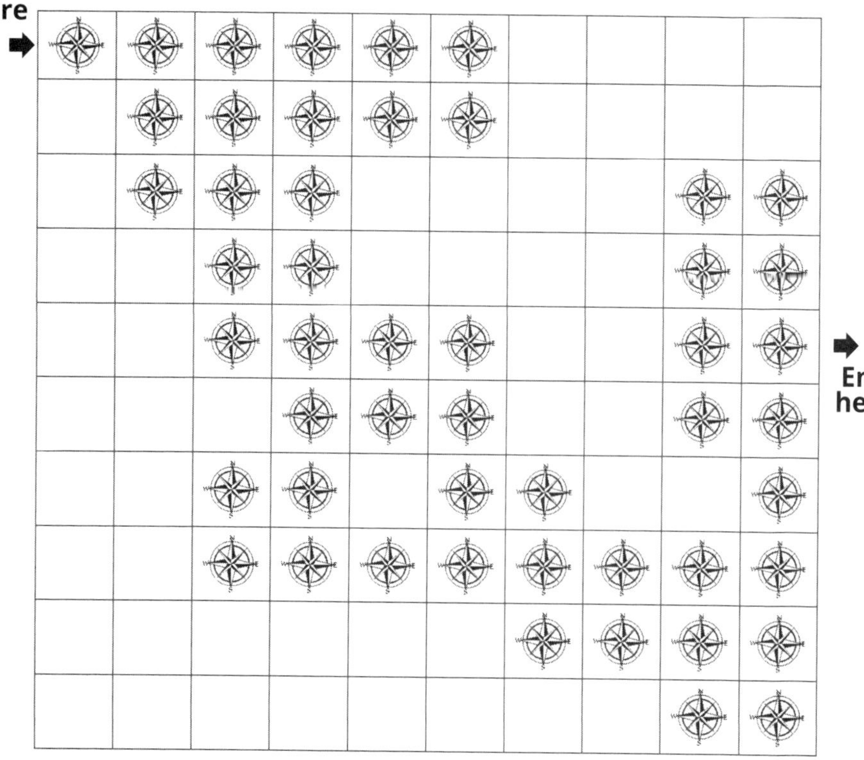

End here

> ***Dear God, sometimes I want to do everything myself. I think I know what's best for me, but that's not true. Help me to look to you to guide my steps and my life.***

Using the message below, break the code and figure out which letter corresponds to which number.

	12	8		2			16		26	25		20
A	B	C	D	E	F	G	H	I	J	K	L	M
9			24		1					23		22
N	O	P	Q	R	S	T	U	V	W	X	Y	Z

10 4 1 2   7 2 15 7 19 2   8 3 9
_ _ _ _   _ _ _ _ _ _   _ _ _

3 19 1 15   19 4 1 5 2 9   3 9 14
_ _ _ _   _ _ _ _ _ _   _ _ _

19 2 3 6 9   2 13 2 9   5 16 2 18
_ _ _ _ _ ; _ _ _ _   _ _ _ _

8 3 9   21 4 9 14   11 15 15 14
_ _ _   _ _ _ _   _ _ _ _

3 14 13 4 8 2   4 9   5 16 2 1 2
_ _ _ _ _ _   _ _   _ _ _ _ _

10 15 6 14 1
_ _ _ _ _ .

Answer on page 124

P B
R Y
C K
P W A E F
U M I S C X S S U T
K O Q U U W E O L S D C J Q G
E F D M B P E G A N A M I D W M X U
R Z V P C D E D I V O R P N V C I
P K T O V E C C J P Q J E C W X D
C H R Y L I Q H C X J D C J B E J G
H M T H I J I P E N D I M T L M X P T
N I I V L E S N U O C P N O G J R P R O
J A E I R Z E N L J N O I T U A C B O K
B B E K H R V L D J Z M W N W K M E J D N B H W B Z P K
G B J M B A M I C N R L O Q Q G N B F N F O X C F B S J
M B N Z G Z R Q R C H U E B N E S Z E K
G D A F P A I N S T R U C T V M X K W A
G S O N W H T C E D F D T Q W M J T Q
B O O Y B N E Q H L Z R E B O E C X
R T V L S Q E H E J R A Z S C P U
O I C A A P K T A L U K Z M E Q T
O U I C C I U Q D Z O Q P G R N U
O B U Q E S I V R E P U S D P
P R C E O E F F S N
S C F E I
A H
T J
E P

WORD LIST

ADVOCATE	EXHORT	NAVIGATE
CAUTION	GUIDE	PROVIDE
COUNSEL	INPUT	RECOMMEND
DELIVER	INSTRUCT	SUPERVISE
DIRECT	MANAGE	SUPPORT

Find your way to the center of the maze.

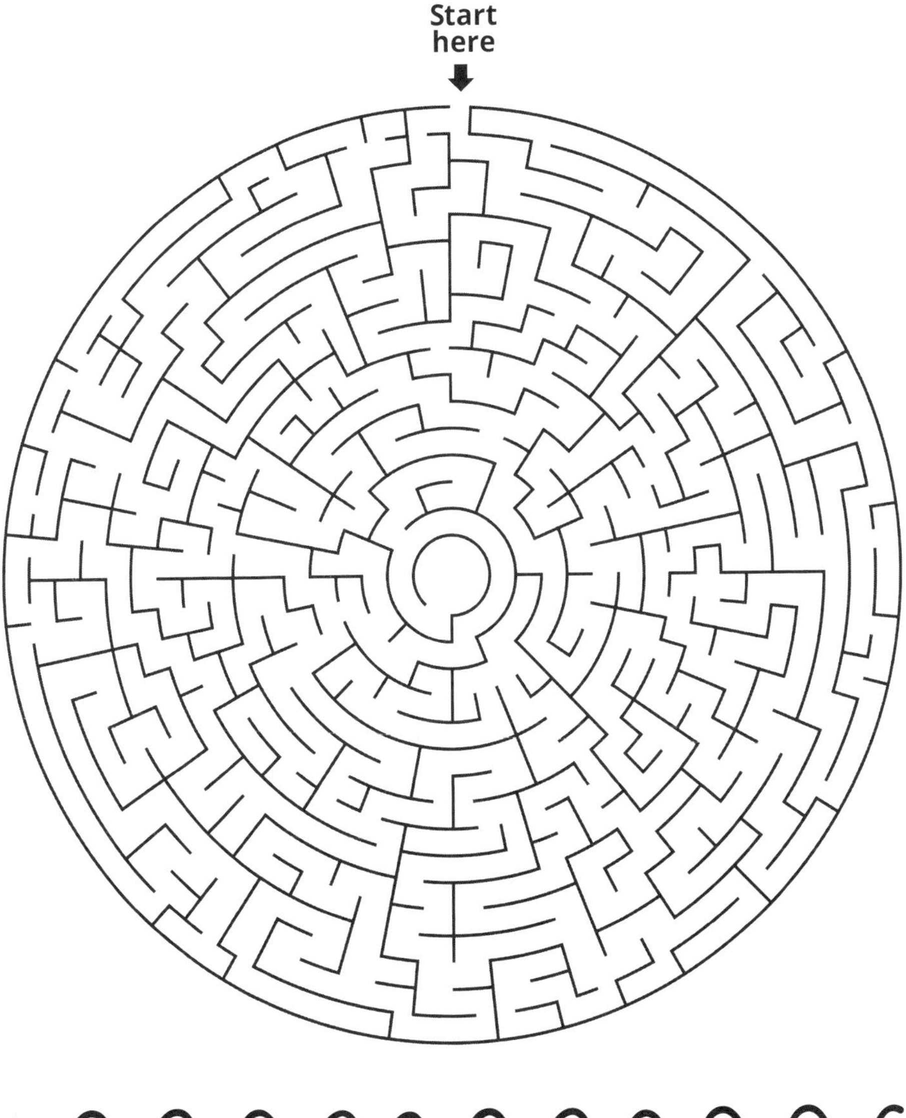

HIGHLIGHT

AT THE BEACH!

Sandy beaches are made mostly of silica.

•

The slope of the beach depends on whether it is made up of sand or shingle and if the waves are constructive or destructive.

•

Shorelines protected from wind and waves tend to have finer sand.

•

The longest beach in the world is Praia do Cassino in Rio Grande, Brazil. It is about 132 miles long.

•

Fraser Island off the coast of Australia is the largest sand island in the world.

•

A beach is not an ideal place for most animals to live because the environment changes so often.

•

The tallest sandcastle on record was made in Connecticut. It stood 37 feet 10 inches tall.

•

The ocean covers 71% of the earth's surface.

•

More than twice the number of people visit America's coasts and beaches than people visiting all state and national parks combined.

Unscramble the following words to figure out the message.

E W   C N A   K E A M

___ ___   ___ ___ ___   ___ ___ ___ ___

R U O   N L A P S

___ ___ ___   ___ ___ ___ ___ ___,

T U B   H E T   R O D L

___ ___ ___   ___ ___ ___   ___ ___ ___ ___

T R M E D E I E S N

___ ___ ___ ___ ___ ___ ___ ___ ___ ___

U R O   T P E S S

___ ___ ___   ___ ___ ___ ___ ___.

Answer on page 124

What 10 places would you most like to visit?

1 ____________________

2 ____________________

3 ____________________

4 ____________________

5 ____________________

6 ____________________

7 ____________________

8 ____________________

9 ____________________

10 ____________________

THANKFULNESS

Give thanks as you enter the gates of his temple. Give praise as you enter its courtyards. Give thanks to him and praise his name.

PSALM 100:4 NIRV

It is easy to be thankful when everything is going well. But it can be hard to be thankful when life is hard. We always have a choice. We can be grumpy when things are wrong, or we can choose thankfulness.

When you choose to be thankful, you see all the good things rather than the bad. The next time you want to complain about dinner, be thankful that you have food. When you are mad with a family member, be thankful that God placed you in a family.

As you travel, you might be even more aware of everything you can be thankful for. Whether you are visiting places where there are many poor people, or you are at a beautiful resort, find ways to thank God for all he has blessed you with.

						Q	K	U	H	C	F	F	C						
				K	L	V	R	L	K	K	K	L	A	N	V				
			C	M	A	H	A	L	O	M	U	S	J	B	A	T			
		A	A	T	H			Y	G	D	V			M	I	X	B		
	Q	D	A	U	D			Q	R	U	Z			E	C	S	A	H	
	H	I	V	E	V			K	A	D	O			R	Q	B	A	P	
W	C	N	N	W	T			K	C	A	G			C	I	G	D	P	G
A	L	B	P	U	M			C	I	T	Y			I	Z	L	H	O	S
G	R	A	Z	I	E			C	A	Y	E			N	H	P	A	Z	A
V	J	H	K	K	D	I	N	A	S	D	A	H	A	M	E	C	N	N	B
K	K	A	T	N	N	T	H	D	V	N	O	I	N	Y	J	K	Y	O	B
B	S	S	E	N	Y	I	D	G	M	Y	M	T	I	C	O	K	A	P	K
X	C	M		O	T	S	I	R	A	H	F	E	Y	L	D		V	P	T
J	U	A			I	S	M	R	C	J	J	R	U	Q			A	H	A
	L	G	O			D	L	O	O	U	N	D	Y			B	A	U	
	U	M	R	Z											S	N	D	A	
		J	L	Z	G									Z	K	I	D		
			A	R	I	G	A	T	O	A	W	F	I	Y	Q	O			
				D	A	N	K	E	S	E	H	R	O	N	Z				
						X	J	G	A	U	N	U	B						

Find the different ways to say "thank you" in the word search above.

ARIGATO	GAMSAHABNIDA	MERCI
DANKE SEHR	GRACIAS	SPASIBA
DHANYAVAAD	GRAZIE	TAKK
DO JEH	MAHADSANID	THANK YOU
EFHARISTO	MAHALO	TODA

Dear God, you are so good! Thank you for this day. Thank you for my friends and family. Thank you for the beautiful world you created. Help me to give you thanks in all I say and do instead of complaining. You are the reason for every blessing in my life.

Replacing one letter at a time, change WHINE to THANK!

WHINE

_ _ _ _ _ period of time

_ _ _ _ _ large ocean mammal

_ _ _ _ _ type of rock

_ _ _ _ _ a thick milky drink

_ _ _ _ _ a boy's name

_ _ _ _ _ to hit a golf ball incorrectly

THANK

Answer on page 125

ACROSS

2. When you travel from one place to another, it might be called a ...
5. Time away from school or work
7. The person who shows you around on your trip (4, 5)
9. What you put your things in when traveling
10. What you need to get on a plane, train, bus, etc.
11. What people hunt for using a map with an X
12. To look around a new place

DOWN

1. If you don't know where you are, you might be ...
3. A word you say to someone who is going on a trip
4. What you need to show you how to get somewhere
6. What you buy to cover any losses on your trip
8. Customs, traditions, and beliefs of certain people

Answer on page 125

Find your way to the center of the maze.

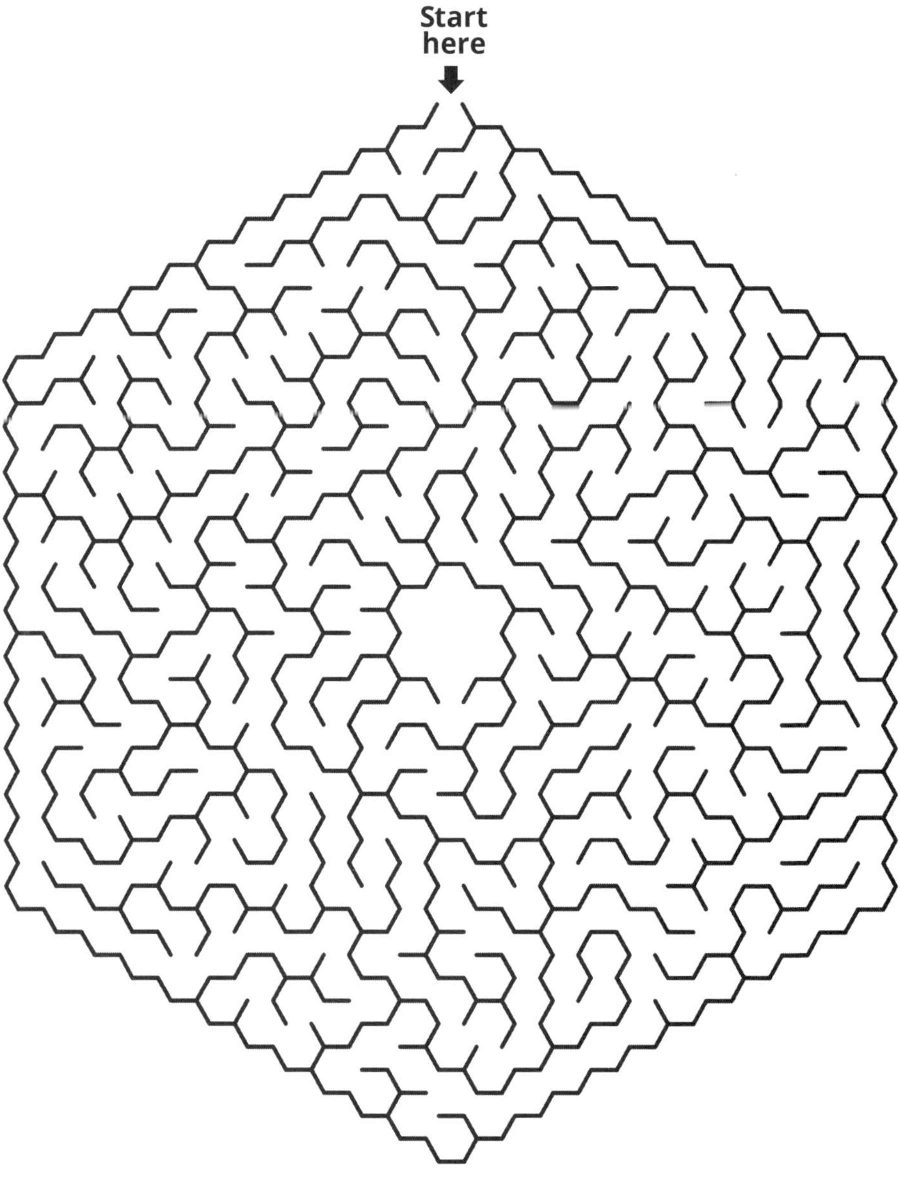

Use the code below to read the secret message.

◎	⅄	☼	□	🌢	✓	❖	◆	✿	✞	☺	✎	♒
A	B	C	D	E	F	G	H	I	J	K	L	M

★	↑	↓	●	⌘	☸	✖	⁂	▣	✸	✂	※	❄
N	O	P	Q	R	S	T	U	V	W	X	Y	Z

⌘ 🌢 ✞ ↑ ✿ ☼ 🌢

___ ___ ___ ___ ___ ___ ___

◎ ✎ ✸ ◎ ※ ☸   ↓ ⌘ ◎ ※

___ ___ ___ ___ ___ ___ ,   ___ ___ ___ ___

☼ ↑ ★ ✖ ✿ ★ ⁂ ◎ ✎ ✎ ※

___ ___ ___ ___ ___ ___ ___ ___ ___ ___ ___ ,

❖ ✿ ▣ 🌢   ✖ ◆ ◎ ★ ☺ ☸

___ ___ ___ ___   ___ ___ ___ ___ ___ ___

✿ ★   ◎ ✎ ✎

___ ___   ___ ___ ___

☼ ✿ ⌘ ☼ ⁂ ♒ ☸ ✖ ◎ ★ ☼ 🌢 ☸

___ ___ ___ ___ ___ ___ ___ ___ ___ ___ ___ ___ ___ .

Answer on page 125

HIGHLIGHT

TRAIN TRIP!

70% of all train trips in England either start or finish in London.

•

The longest stretch of perfectly straight railway track is in Australia. It is 297 miles.

•

Grand Central Station in New York has 44 passenger platforms.

•

Trains are one of the most eco-friendly ways you can travel.

•

Some trains can reach speeds of over 340 miles per hour.

•

The London Underground was the world's first underground railroad.

•

India has one of the largest and busiest railroad systems in the world. It has more than 71,500 miles of track, which could circle the earth almost three times.

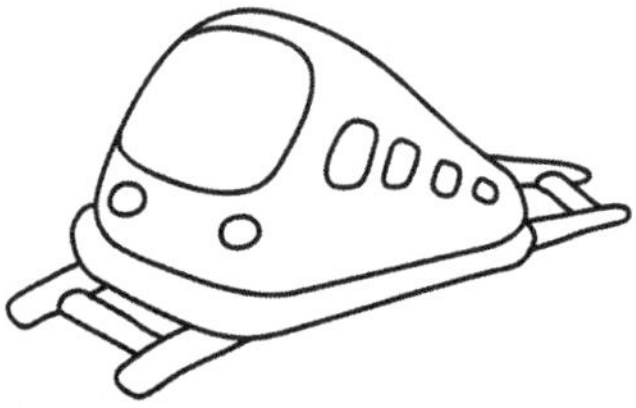

Which two pictures are exactly the same?

Answer on page 125

Use the letters in the word

THANKS

to list some things you are thankful for.

T ______________________________

H ______________________________

A ______________________________

N ______________________________

K ______________________________

S ______________________________

QUIET

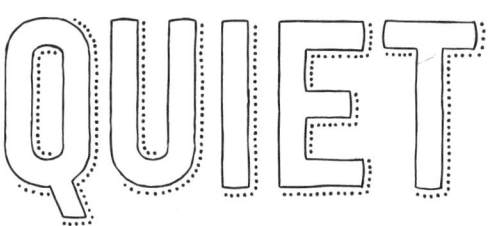

Then Jesus said, "Let's go off by ourselves to a quiet place and rest awhile." He said this because there were so many people coming and going that Jesus and his apostles didn't even have time to eat.

MARK 6:31 NLT

Airports, train stations, tourist spots, and even the backseat of a car can be crowded and noisy. Have you ever felt like you just wanted to get away from all the noise and people? Jesus felt like this too! He encouraged the disciples to get away from the crowds with him.

God knows that there are times when you just need to find a quiet place and take a break from all the activity. It's good to settle your heart and mind for a little while each day.

When you travel, you might have lots of opportunities to rest, or you might feel even busier than normal. Can you find a place to be peaceful, just for a few minutes, today? Take some time to talk to God on your own. Thank him for the beautiful things around you and ask him to fill you with peace.

Find your way to the center of the maze.

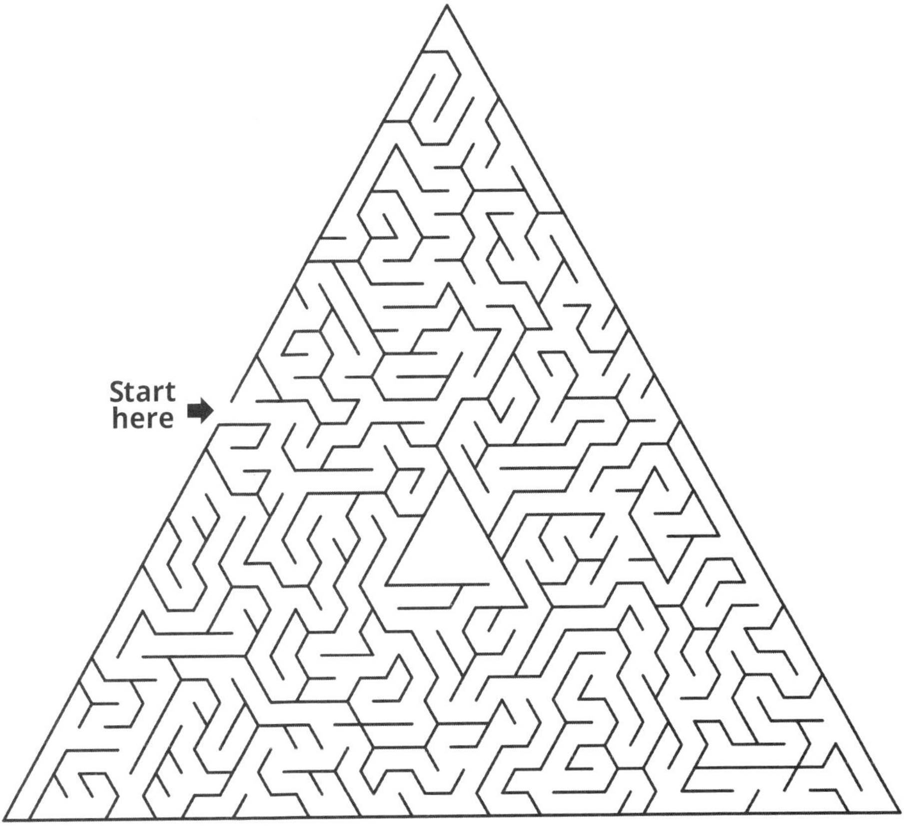

Dear God, it's easy to fill my head with noise. I like to listen to music, talk with my friends, play games, and watch movies. But it's good to just sit and be quiet sometimes. Teach me to be quiet more so I can hear your voice.

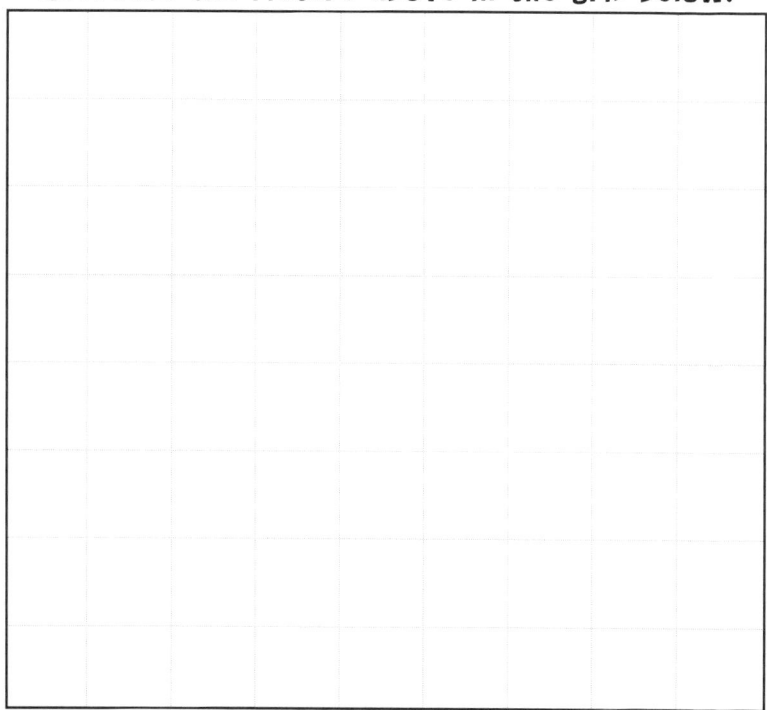

Recreate the picture above in the grid below.

Use the Pictures to help you figure out the secret message.

 2 

There is a __________ ______ ___________ apart

 2 

and a ___________ ________ _________ together.

 2  

There is a __________ _______ ________ _______________

 2 

and a ___________ ________ __________________.

Answer on page 125

										W										
									B	M	A									
								B	F	J	I	I								
							R	K	R	C	Z	P	V							
						A	M	P	E	X	C	F	N	I						
					Z	Q	P	R	N	E	Y	V	U	W	L					
				I	K	S	H	G	C	P	C	Q	D	H	I	O				
			L	C	N	W	Y	U	H	P	P	S	O	O	C	Y	B			
		P	J	R	R	S	K	T	G	J	V	P	S	C	I	V	R	R		
	J	J	E	P	S	F	R	S	U	O	E	U	R	U	G	U	A	Y	Q	
E	M	I	W	R	J	F	Z	G	I	I	N	M	F	D	B	M	H	Y	Z	Z
			B	S	U				A	E	E				P	X	R			
			Y	U	A				N	Z	Z				E	A	H			
			I	R	W				A	T	U				B	N	F			
			R	I	H				O	O	E				J	I	Q			
			O	N	G	U	Y	A	N	A	L	U	Q	V	U	T	V			
			D	A	X	V	O	Q	Z	C	A	A	L	Y	T	N	P			
			A	M	G	P	Z	K	E	C	B	I	M	A	Y	E	L			
			U	E	I	Y	L	W				B	X	U	Q	G	X			
			C	C	H	I	L	E				M	Y	G	A	R	V			
			E	O	T	P	I	D				O	H	A	K	A	T			
			J	I	D	Y	V	Q				L	P	R	L	B	M			
			T	U	Y	E	O	N				O	X	A	E	D	J			
			G	E	Y	Y	T	U				C	W	P	O	Y	L			

Find the countries in South America!

ARGENTINA
BOLIVIA
BRAZIL
CHILE
COLOMBIA
ECUADOR
FRENCH GUIANA
GUYANA
PARAGUAY
PERU
SURINAME
URUGUAY
VENEZUELA

HIGHLIGHT

CABIN GETAWAY!

Some of the earliest log cabins in North America were built in the 1600s.

•

Seven of the US presidents were either born in or have lived in a log cabin.

•

One cabin built in Finland is estimated to be about 4,000 years old.

•

The largest cabin in the world is 26,000 square feet. It has 23 bedrooms and 13 bathrooms and is located in Michigan.

•

Lincoln Logs, building toys resembling logs that you stack to create cabins, were first sold in 1916. That's over 100 years ago!

Unscramble the words to figure out the secret message.

H O S E T   H O W   R E A

_ _ _ _ _   _ _ _   _ _ _

R E C F U A L   B T A U O

_ _ _ _ _ _ _   _ _ _ _ _

T H A W   H T Y E   Y A S

_ _ _ _   _ _ _ _   _ _ _

E K E P   M E V H E S L T E S

_ _ _ _   _ _ _ _ _ _ _ _ _ _

U T O   F O   R U O T B E L

_ _ _   _ _   _ _ _ _ _ _ _.

Answer on page 125

Spot the ten Differences Between the two Pictures.

Spend some quiet time with God. Write down the things you hear him saying to you.

PROTECTION

The LORD keeps you from all harm
and watches over your life.
The LORD keeps watch over you
as you come and go, both now
and forever.

PSALM 121:7-8 NLT

Have you ever seen a bird in a cage with a cat sitting outside watching the bird? If there were no cage, the bird might be really afraid, but it knows it is safe inside the cage. You might feel the same way at the zoo. The bears behind the glass or lions in the enclosure are fun to watch as long as you're on the right side of the barrier. If you found yourself on the other side, it might not be so fun!

We can feel strong and sure in life because we have the best protection of all—Jesus. He is faithful, and he promises to take care of us. Sometimes he doesn't do the things we want him to do, but we can be sure that he has our very best in mind.

When you are feeling a little uncertain, remind yourself that God is your protection and your help.

Dear God, I feel safe knowing you are always watching over me. I never have to fear because you are my defender. Help me to think of you the next time I am afraid.

Make 20 new words out of **PROTECT**.

Only use each letter once.

P _ _ _ _ _	P _ _ _
C _ _ _ _	R _ _ _
O _ _ _ _	R _ _ _
O _ _ _ _	T _ _ _
T _ _ _ _	T _ _ _
C _ _ _	C _ _
C _ _ _	C _ _
C _ _ _	O _ _
P _ _ _	P _ _
P _ _ _	P _ _

Answer on page 125

Hidden in the picture below are 10 airplanes. See if you can find them.

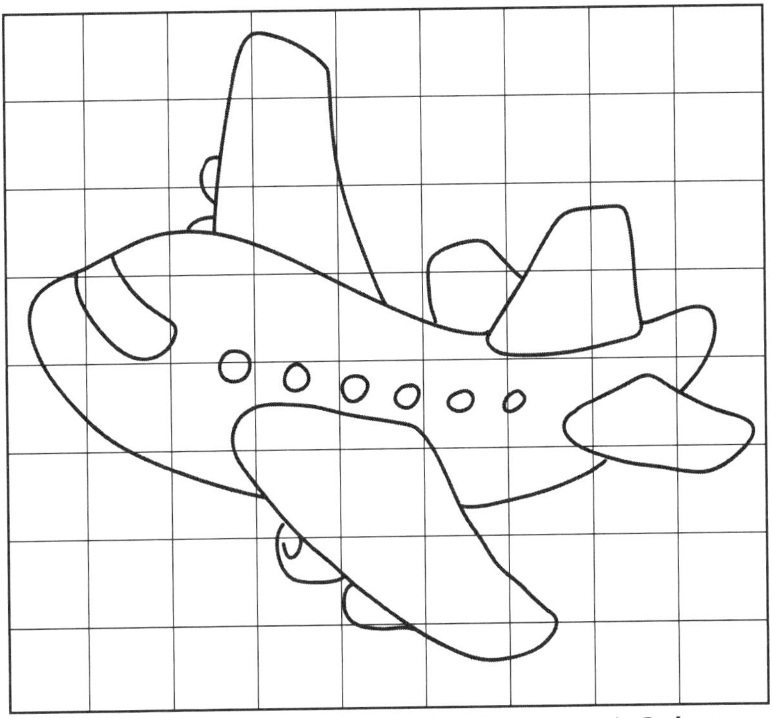

Recreate the picture above in the grid below.

Y	U	X	X	A	T	D	J	Y	D	G	Y	G	H	J	G	D	L	A	F
I	Y	H	O	C	I	X	E	M	Y	K	S	J	A	Y	M	V	X	D	D
L	N	T	G	L	X	V	T	S	O	Z	T	H	C	H	R	T	C	B	F
C	W	F	H	D	P	U	L	U	B	B	O	X	I	H	U	S	G	E	X
I	H	A	S	X	I	Q	V	L	I	E	R	R	R	P	I	A	G	L	N
L	D	C	U	H	O	N	D	U	R	A	S	K	A	C	T	V	G	I	L
B	A	B	P	G	P	N	P	X	E	D	Y	L	T	Q	I	Q	T	Z	P
U	B	A	T	W	A	R	X	I	E	R	M	P	S	S	A	G	O	E	V
P	R	V	E	B	F	R	F	C	U	U	T	C	O	R	H	Z	D	S	J
E	K	T	D	H	X	R	A	Q	A	B	G	U	C	Y	V	A	U	E	H
R	O	C	A	N	A	D	A	C	Q	J	D	U	T	V	O	A	L	K	Y
N	Q	V	V	O	J	K	J	N	I	Z	K	Z	A	I	M	S	Y	F	L
A	N	O	T	M	Z	J	Y	N	B	N	E	Y	C	T	A	R	Q	K	H
C	S	E	T	A	T	S	D	E	T	I	N	U	D	L	E	L	W	P	S
I	T	M	I	W	Q	C	R	I	Z	H	M	K	V	R	F	M	Q	X	C
N	T	I	Z	G	U	R	H	K	O	L	X	A	C	V	R	T	A	C	M
I	A	B	L	B	Y	Q	N	I	J	Z	D	W	Z	L	B	U	V	L	E
M	W	Q	A	J	D	P	E	F	W	O	E	J	U	H	Z	O	Z	O	A
O	A	M	A	N	A	P	J	H	R	B	O	Y	Y	X	K	H	O	W	W
D	R	M	V	A	A	L	C	L	R	X	Q	O	N	X	H	A	X	H	N

Find these countries in North & Central America and the Caribbean.

BELIZE
CANADA
COSTA RICA
CUBA
DOMINICAN REPUBLIC
EL SALVADOR
GUATEMALA
HAITI
HONDURAS
MEXICO
NICARAGUA
PANAMA
UNITED STATES

Find your way to the center of the maze.

HIGHLIGHT

CAMPING!

Tents are the most popular type of shelter when people go camping.

•

The average camper is 35 years old.

•

There are about 13,000 campgrounds in the USA.

•

The most common camping purchase is a flashlight.

•

On average, people camp for less than three nights.

•

About 40 million people go camping in the United States each year.

•

Crickets can tell you the temperature! Count the number of chirps you hear in 14 seconds. Add 40 to that number and you'll have the temperature in Fahrenheit.

Draw a line from the beginning to the end that passes through each box with a TENT in it once. The line can go up, down, left, or right, but cannot go diagonal.

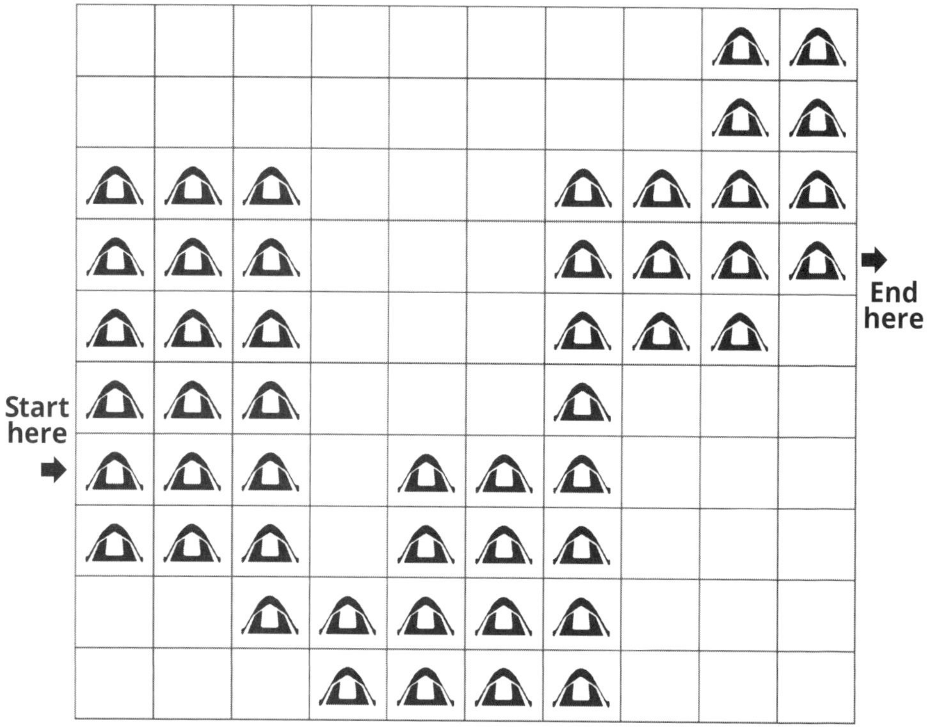

Write Down three things you are afraid of and then write how God protects you.

1

2

3

RESPECT

Trust in your leaders. Put yourselves under their authority. Do this, because they keep watch over you. They know they are accountable to God for everything they do. Do this, so that their work will be a joy. If you make their work a heavy load, it won't do you any good.

Hebrews 13:17 NIRV

Who is older than you are? Your parents, teachers, babysitters, siblings? When you are young, there are a lot of people older than you. Think about how much older they are: 10 years, 20 years, 30 years, or maybe even more!

Older people know more than you do because they have experienced life for longer than you have. Showing respect for your leaders means that you take the time to listen to what they have to say, and you consider them before you go ahead and do things for yourself.

Listen to your teachers, obey your parents, offer an elderly person your seat or hold the door open for them. God will reward you when you show respect to those around you.

Dear God, sometimes I am disrespectful when I disagree with other people or when I don't get my way. You say to show respect for all people and to especially respect and obey my leaders, like parents and teachers. Help me to be more respectful to everyone in my life, so they can see the love and respect I have for you.

TOP 10 MOST POPULAR VACATION SPOTS IN THE WORLD:

#10
NEW YORK CITY, USA

#9
DUBAI, UAE

#8
GRAND CANYON, USA

#7
PHUKET, THAILAND

#6
SOUTH ISLAND, NEW ZEALAND

#5
LONDON, ENGLAND

#4
TAHITI, FRENCH POLYNESIA

#3
ROME, ITALY

#2
YELLOWSTONE, USA

#1
PARIS, FRANCE

Use the alphabet code below to figure out the secret message.

1	2	3	4	5	6	7	8	9	10	11	12	13
A	B	C	D	E	F	G	H	I	J	K	L	M

14	15	16	17	18	19	20	21	22	23	24	25	26
N	O	P	Q	R	S	T	U	V	W	X	Y	Z

4 15 14 ' 20   4 15   1 14 25 20 8 9 14 7

15 14 12 25   20 15   7 5 20

1 8 5 1 4 .   4 15 14 ' 20   4 15   9 20

2 5 3 1 21 19 5   25 15 21   1 18 5

16 18 15 21 4 .   9 14 19 20 5 1 4 ,   2 5

8 21 13 2 12 5 .   22 1 12 21 5

15 20 8 5 18 19   13 15 18 5   20 8 1 14

25 15 21 18 19 5 12 22 5 19 .

Answer on page 125

Which traveler goes to what continent?

Answer on page 126

		X	J	X	Q	X	F	H				N	O	R	W	A	Y	S		
		D	X	S	P	Z	M	Z	V		H	S	Y	U	G	S	E	H		
U	M		V	N	E	A	Q	K	S		Z	N	Z	W	C	Z	E		L	L
W	I	C	E	L	A	N	D	C	I		L	L	Y	Q	Z	F	U	L	X	S
P	N	J	G	Q	Z	X	O	R	V		T	M	S	X	S	G	C	L	A	Q
G	O	U	F	D	E	T	D	W	A		T	J	M	V	K	X	O	V	D	W
H	D	V	L	N	L	J	V	B	W		U	Y	D	K	L	T	U	N	R	V
Z	K	X	M	A	L	A	D	B	K	R	A	M	N	E	D	R	A	V	O	Y
W	I	W	N	L	L	T	X	Q	O	E	R	H	A	K	P	L	C	O	A	A
	O	D	Q	T	K	I	H	U	N	N	P	X	L	V	E	L	B	G	J	
						K	T	G	O	N	F	J	N	R						
	M	M	I	I	O	U	L	H	Z	X	X	A	I	Y	A	T	P	Z	Q	
L	O	L	T	F	F	A	L	J	U	T	G	N	F	Z	H	Y	C	X	E	L
G	A	Q	A	J	N	K	X	F	N	A	R	G	N	Q	W	C	V	Z	C	A
I	H	I	I	D	E	R	P	V	N	E	N	G	A	B	M	X	K	H	H	T
B	A	T	N	J	G	X	R	G	H		G	I	D	N	A	L	E	R	I	V
J	H	B	O	E	M	T	F	T	J		H	O	A	T	J	W	O	W	K	I
G	D	W	T	E	K	W	R	Q	N		R	S	K	Y	O	H	Y	L	J	A
B	O		S	W	I	O	N	Q	A		F	A	R	L	E	A	I		E	Q
		X	E	P	N	C	G	T	V		E	Z	N	S	G	A	U	W		
		S	N	E	D	E	W	S				F	V	G	J	J	N	D		

Find the Northern European countries in the word search above.

DENMARK
ENGLAND
ESTONIA
FINLAND
ICELAND
IRELAND
LATVIA
LITHUANIA
NORTHERN IRELAND
NORWAY
SCOTLAND
SWEDEN
WALES

Find your way through the maze.

Start here

End here

Use the Pictures to help you figure out the secret message.

 – M + SH   4    – B

__________ respect __________ __________ people:

__________ the __________ and __________

    – R + G

of God's __________, respect __________

honor the __________.

Answer on page 126

HIGHLIGHT

SIGHT SEEING!

Here were the ten most popular tourist attractions in 2018:

1. Colosseum, Rome
2. The Vatican Museums, Rome
3. The Statue of Liberty, New York City
4. The Louvre Museum, Paris
5. Eiffel Tower, Paris
6. Basilica, Barcelona
7. Golden Gate Bridge, San Francisco
8. Stonehenge, Wiltshire
9. Palace of Versailles, Versailles
10. The Grand Canal, Venice

•

London, England draws more international visitors than any other city on the planet.

•

The Golden Gate Bridge is actually painted "international orange."

•

Big Ben is the name of the clock's bell, not the tower itself. The tower is called the Clock Tower.

•

Australia has more than 10,000 beaches—the most of any other country.

•

Six million cubic feet of water pour into Niagara Falls every minute – that's enough to fill a million bathtubs to the top in sixty seconds.

What five people do you respect most in life? How can you show each of them respect?

1

2

3

4

5

HELPFULNESS

A cheerful look brings joy to the heart; good news makes for good health.

PROVERBS 15:30 NLT

Little things are important. Offer a smile to someone who isn't nice to you. Say a prayer for a friend who is having a bad day. Have compassion on someone who is complaining. These little acts of helpfulness can change a person's day.

Do you ever feel like God makes you notice certain people? He does that for a reason! Your smile might be the first smile they have gotten in a long time. Your compliment could boost their confidence for the rest of the day. Your offer to help might be just what they need to keep going.

Choose to look at others with love and be ready to serve them. This will bring joy to their heart and a smile to God's face.

Which two Pictures are exactly the same?

Answer on page 126

Follow the lines to find out who will help in what way.

Answer on page 126

ACROSS

3. A deep valley with steep sides
7. Elevation of the earth rising to a summit
8. A body of land surrounded by water
10. A natural stream of water
11. A stretch of sand or pebbles along a shore

DOWN

1. A depression between mountains
2. A mountain that expels lava
4. An area of flat land
5. The large body of salt water that covers 3/4 of the earth
6. An extended mass of ice
9. A body of water surrounded by land
10. A ridge of rocks or sand at the surface of the water

Answer on page 126

Find your way to the center of the maze.

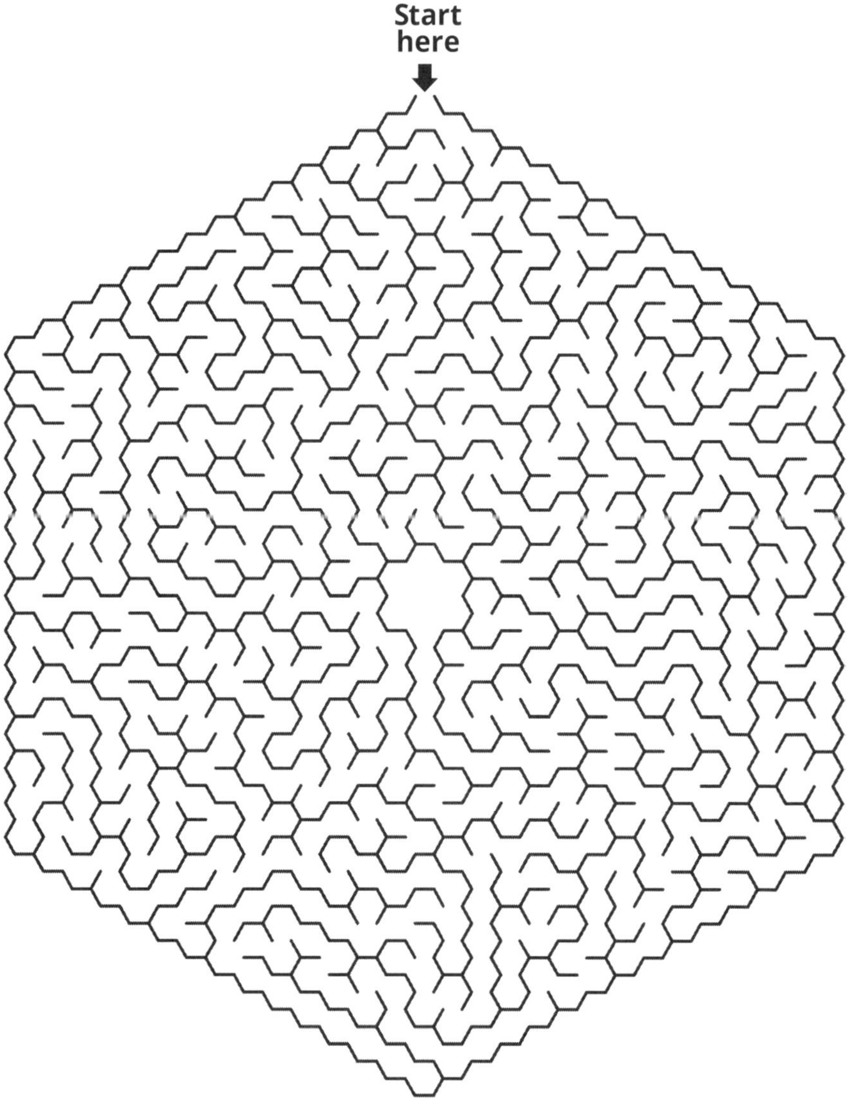

Dear God, it feels good to receive help, but you say it is better to serve others instead. That is a good reminder. I want to love and help people who have less than I do.

Use the code below to read the secret message.

◎	⅄	☼	□	💧	✓	❖	♦	✿	✝	☺	✎	♒
A	B	C	D	E	F	G	H	I	J	K	L	M

★	↑	↓	●	⌘	☸	✕	⁂	▣	✸	✂	※	❄
N	O	P	Q	R	S	T	U	V	W	X	Y	Z

☸ ♦ ◎ ⌘ 💧   ✸ ✿ ✕ ♦   ✕ ♦ 💧

_ _ _ _ _   _ _ _ _   _ _ _

✎ ↑ ⌘ □ , ☸   ↓ 💧 ↑ ↓ ✎ 💧   ✸ ♦ ↑

_ _ _ _ ' _   _ _ _ _ _ _   _ _ _

◎ ⌘ 💧   ✿ ★   ★ 💧 💧 □

_ _ _   _ _   _ _ _ _ .

✸ 💧 ✎ ☼ ↑ ♒ 💧   ↑ ✕ ♦ 💧 ⌘ ☸

_ _ _ _ _ _ _   _ _ _ _ _ _

✿ ★ ✕ ↑   ※ ↑ ⁂ ⌘   ♦ ↑ ♒ 💧 ☸

_ _ _ _   _ _ _ _   _ _ _ _ _ .

Answer on page 126

HIGHLIGHT

MISSIONS TRIP!

One of the most important things you can do on a missions trip is to encourage the missionaries you visit. Serve them with your heart and your hands, and you'll do a world of good!

•

If you are visiting missionaries, don't complain about something you have to do for a week to people who have to do that work every day.

•

Expect to learn something; don't think you already know it all.

•

Don't expect to change the world but expect to be changed.

•

Make real connections with the people you are visiting. Cause them to feel like they are seen, heard, and loved.

•

Take an interest in the culture. Try their food. Listen to their music. Enjoy who they are as people.

•

About 2 million people in America participate in missions trips every year.

W Y B F U
D B C U B L U   R D N Q N X
R O O Z R D I   K F A D I R F
N X Q B B X S   L M T Z T O B B
A E N E V J Z   C E S T E Q L A W
T K B K A O U   N X I Q D X S E M
S I P I X D Y   H P K D A E P Z U
I S O S W X A   W F I J R M O F R
N V B T U P I   O K J B A A B X B
A N D A J E R   G G A P B J A N G
H X E N A I Y D T A E W S S U
G L R Z S Q S J M X C A Q
F O H W D V I V E U U
A F J E R L F D M
Y V N B A Q L I H
B Z A G T I D A S T F
C N T K E V A R E U U M F
M G S H S K E A D Y I R U Z Z
T R I B G Z F B A   V V K H J L I
L D K S O M G I L   M E N T U O X
I R A N R F A A G   Y M O I G X D
Y U P P W A F N N   F Y N A T M W
M I E C A   O F A W J K H
G   J L B   V M B U J N Z
Z   Y G   M N E K S I
T   M   Y G L Q N
P W M Y   F H A D
Q A R I   K O I
J Z M   S A
A C   R

Find the South, West, and Central Asia countries in the word search below.

AFGHANISTAN
BANGLADESH
INDIA
IRAN
IRAQ
ISRAEL
KUWAIT
LEBANON
PAKISTAN
SAUDI ARABIA
SYRIA
TAJIKISTAN
TURKEY
UNITED ARAB EMIRATES
UZBEKISTAN

Use the word

HELP

to share how you can help the people around you.

H

E

L

P

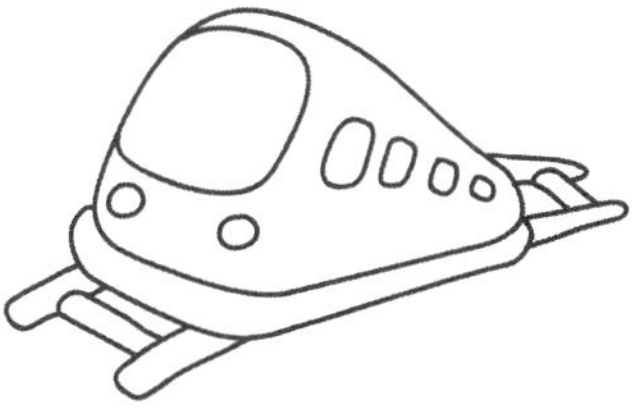

ENJOYMENT

Your unfailing love is
better than life itself;
how I praise you!
Psalm 63:3 NLT

What are your favorite things in life? Is it your bike, or perhaps it's ice cream, a roller-coaster, discovering something new, or just being with friends? It might be all of these!

Did you know that God created enjoyment? He wanted us to have fun in life because he loves us. This verse says that God's love is even better than life. That's pretty awesome.

The next time you are really enjoying something that you love, remember that God created it for you. And then remember to thank him for it.

Dear God, thank you for the ability to enjoy everything around me. Thank you for letting me laugh with my friends and family and smile at all the wonders you have created. I am happy that I belong to you.

Unscramble the letters to reveal different countries in Western & Eastern Europe.

U T A I S R A _ _ _ _ _ _ _

G B L U E I M _ _ _ _ _ _ _

A N F C R E _ _ _ _ _ _

R E M Y N G A _ _ _ _ _ _ _

D N T L E N R H A E S _ _ _ _ _ _ _ _ _ _ _

D N R I S T E W Z L A _ _ _ _ _ _ _ _ _ _ _

U I A B L R G A _ _ _ _ _ _ _ _

H G R U A N Y _ _ _ _ _ _ _

N L P A D O _ _ _ _ _ _

A O I R M N A _ _ _ _ _ _ _

R S I U S A _ _ _ _ _ _

I K A U R E N _ _ _ _ _ _ _

Answer on page 126

Use the code below to read the secret message.

◎	⅄	☼	☐	💧	✓	❖	♦	✿	✞	☺	✎	≋
A	B	C	D	E	F	G	H	I	J	K	L	M

★	↑	↓	●	⌘	☸	✕	⁂	▣	✸	✂	※	❄
N	O	P	Q	R	S	T	U	V	W	X	Y	Z

◎ ✎ ✸ ◎ ※ ☸   ⅄ 💧   ✞ ↑ ※ ✓ ⁂ ✎

___ ___ ___ ___ ___ ___   ___ ___   ___ ___ ___ ___ ___ ___

⅄ 💧 ☼ ◎ ⁂ ☸ 💧   ※ ↑ ⁂

___ ___ ___ ___ ___ ___ ___   ___ ___ ___

⅄ 💧 ✎ ↑ ★ ❖   ✕ ↑   ✕ ♦ 💧

___ ___ ___ ___ ___ ___   ___ ___   ___ ___ ___

✎ ↑ ⌘ ☐   ✿   ✸ ✿ ✎ ✎   ☸ ◎ ※

___ ___ ___ ___ .   ___   ___ ___ ___ ___   ___ ___ ___

✿ ✕   ◎ ❖ ◎ ✿ ★   ⅄ 💧

___ ___   ___ ___ ___ ___ ___   ___ ___

✞ ↑ ※ ✓ ⁂ ✎

___ ___ ___ ___ ___ ___ !

Answer on page 127

Find your way through the maze.

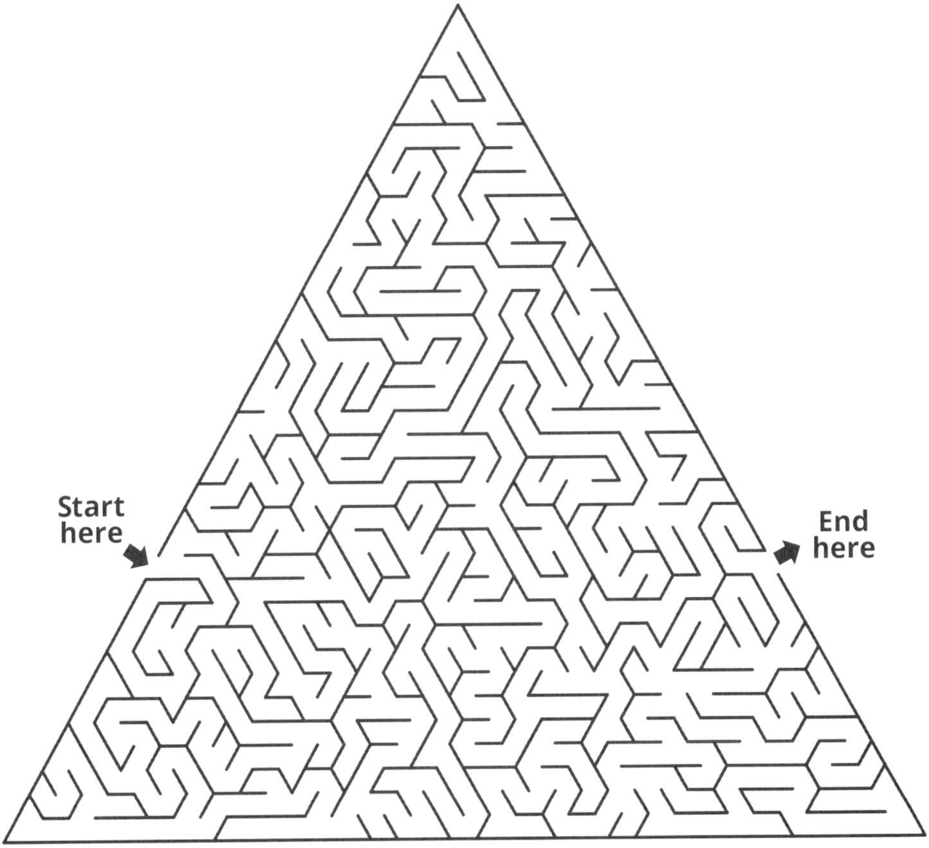

A

T

M L Y

I A T

U I M I P

R O C C D

F L R R N Y S

V A G O A E P

C E G L D A S K I E A C N A L O S M L K S

Q C H D N F S N N T I D I M L P A A A

B E S D H E A E I T J N J G G I N

S E O C R B T A A A M R U N M

G R P B L N X V A Q T E A

R G I A O W C W R V R

A W A B M E Z O O I D

S N J O K D T P L N I I P

T S S M O Z S O I S L O

X Z N S S N P X W T L A W

K I S I R S C A Y O

R A E A Z L E W

P X Y C

P M

Find the countries in the word search below that are all a part of Southern Europe.

ALBANIA	ITALY	SAN MARINO
ANDORRA	MACEDONIA	SERBIA
BOSNIA	MALTA	SLOVENIA
CROATIA	MONTENEGRO	SPAIN
GREECE	PORTUGAL	VATICAN CITY

Use the Pictures to help you figure out the secret message.

  – B + SH

always me

  – KN + L

the ______________ of ______________.

  – H + W  – H + F

__________ ____________ ____________ me

 – B + J   – J 

with ___________ when _____ __________ with _________.

Answer on page 127

HIGHLIGHT

THEME PARKS!

Theme parks were started in Europe during the Middle Ages. They began as fairy gardens.

•

The first modern theme park was built in 1894 in Chicago.

•

The US has more theme parks than any other country in the world.

•

About 270 million people visit theme parks each year.

•

The fastest roller coaster in the world goes from 0 to 150 mph in five seconds.

•

Roller coasters were invented when people began riding mine carts for fun.

•

Walt Disney parks in the US had over 150 million visitors in 2017. That's the most in the world for any theme park.

create your own rollercoaster.

List five things you enjoy the most:

1 ____________________

2 ____________________

3 ____________________

4 ____________________

5 ____________________

COURTESY

"All people will know that you are my followers if you love each other."

John 13:35 NCV

What makes you feel valued? Is it a hug, a smile, a nice note, or a kind word? There are hundreds of ways to show people they have value. One really good way is to be polite. Another word for politeness is *courtesy*.

When we are polite to those around us, we communicate that they are worth something. Courtesy is taking a moment to consider others before doing things for ourselves—letting them choose first, go first, speak first. This can be really hard.

People feel cared for when we show courtesy, and that's a really great way to communicate God's love.

Recreate the picture above in the grid below.

Use the alphabet code below to figure out the secret message.

1	2	3	4	5	6	7	8	9	10	11	12	13
A	B	C	D	E	F	G	H	I	J	K	L	M

14	15	16	17	18	19	20	21	22	23	24	25	26
N	O	P	Q	R	S	T	U	V	W	X	Y	Z

2 5   19 21 18 5   20 8 1 20   14 15

__ __   __ __ __ __   __ __ __ __   __ __

15 14 5   16 1 25 19   2 1 3 11

__ __ __   __ __ __ __   __ __ __ __

23 18 15 14 7   6 15 18   23 18 15 14 7

__ __ __ __ __ .   __ __ __   __ __ __ __ __ .

2 21 20   1 12 23 1 25 19   20 18 25

__ __ __   __ __ __ __ __ __   __ __ __

20 15   4 15   23 8 1 20   9 19

__ __   __ __   __ __ __ __   __ __

7 15 15 4   6 15 18   5 1 3 8

__ __ __ __   __ __ __   __ __ __ __

15 20 8 5 18   1 14 4   6 15 18

__ __ __ __ __   __ __ __   __ __ __

1 12 12   16 5 15 16 12 5

__ __ __   __ __ __ __ __ __ .

Answer on page 127

Who said "hello" in which language?

Answer on page 127

Dear God, I want to build others up and make them feel good. Help me to encourage my friends and family and think about them first. I want to be kind to strangers and help whoever is in need before I help myself.

E

F

H E

D U V W

G I N T X K

N C M A A S S

T O N G A L U V

Q K Z N P K X A N C

A I L A R T S U A E A H

B I E U V V C Q K F M Z V G

O V R A I N O D E L A C W E N

C G U S D N A L S I K O O C E E H

A A E N I U G W E N U A P A P B N K

S O L O M O N I S L A N D S H N F I J I

H

N

D N A L S I S A M T S I R H C C C P D D

N E F R E N C H P O L Y N E S I A I

L P A O M A S N R E T S E W Q X

A I T A B I R I K A W A J F

Find the Australasian countries and territories in the word search below.

AUSTRALIA	NAURU	SOLOMON ISLANDS
CHRISTMAS ISLAND	NEW CALEDONIA	TONGA
COOK ISLANDS	NEW ZEALAND	VANUATU
FIJI	NIUE	WESTERN SAMOA
FRENCH POLYNESIA	PAPAU NEW GUINEA	
KIRIBATI		

Find your way through the maze below.

Start here

End here

HIGHLIGHT

CRUISE!

The largest cruise ship is twice the length of the Washington monument.

•

More cruises depart from Florida than any other state.

•

Adding together all the miles a typical cruise ship sails, they could go around the world almost three and a half times in one year!

•

More than 25 million passengers travel on cruise ships every year.

•

The largest cruise ships are as tall as a 16-storey building.

•

Some cruise ships carry over 5,000 passengers.

•

You might think that a cruise around tropical islands would be the most popular. In a 2018 report, the Caribbean didn't even rank in the top 10! In fact, Glacier Bay, Alaska came first.

Unscramble the words to read the secret message.

R M E E R M B E   O T

_ _ _ _ _ _ _ _   _ _

E C O W L M E   R N S G R A T E S

_ _ _ _ _ _ _   _ _ _ _ _ _ _ _ _ ,

E E C B U A S   M E O S   H O W

_ _ _ _ _ _ _   _ _ _ _   _ _ _

V A H E   E N O D   I H T S

_ _ _ _   _ _ _ _   _ _ _ _

A V H E   W O E L E M C D

_ _ _ _   _ _ _ _ _ _ _ _

G L E A N S   T I O T W H U

_ _ _ _ _ _   _ _ _ _ _ _ _

I N W K O N G   T I

_ _ _ _ _ _ _   _ _ .

Answer on page 127

Use the word POLITE to think of ways you can show courtesy.

P

O

L

I

T

E

GRACE

The Lord shows mercy and is kind.
He does not become angry quickly,
and he has great love.

Psalm 103:8 ICB

Have you ever experienced a moment when you did something wrong and knew you deserved some kind of punishment? You expected someone to be angry, but instead they treated you kindly.

God has that kind of grace for us all the time. He is full of mercy which means that he is kind to us even when we have done something wrong. He doesn't get angry quickly and he makes sure we know he loves us.

When you think of God's grace for you, take the opportunity to show others the same grace. Keep calm when they make you angry and treat them with respect when they yell. Giving people grace usually extinguishes what could be an explosive situation.

Dear Jesus, your grace gave me forgiveness and love. It's what allows me to stay in relationship with you. Help me to act with more grace so I can live like you.

Replacing one letter at a time, Change MEAN to KIND!

MEAN

_ _ _ _ edible seed

_ _ _ _ used to make jewelry

_ _ _ _ force into a curve

_ _ _ _ tie together

KIND

Answer on page 127

J B H T H C W U
N O R T H K O R E A Y S
A I S E N O D N I Y K I I V
A I A A O K M I E S N W
I O N K P R Z Y X N I F D W
A I F M W O M A G U N Z O F
X H X A X Z O D N J R G Z W Q C
C B D S S N Y H M S B A Z V H A
S J G T C Z C S A L G P Y P S M
B F A S O U T H K O R E A S T O U M O B
A M D P S E N I P P I L I H P R Y O T O
X J G A A G I R Z B O V H V Z E G N H D
G S T T N G E A V I E T N A M G N I
U O S Q Y J T M D D E V U O F A
A E F Z P W I C I U H L L O
L R K D C E I L
N A O W Y N N A
C T T H A I L A N D Q A E Q
K C Q Z F T G S F H Y B
A I S Y A L A M

Find the East and Southeast Asia countries in the word search below.

BRUNEI	LAOS	PHILIPPINES
CAMBODIA	MALAYSIA	SINGAPORE
CHINA	MONGOLIA	SOUTH KOREA
INDONESIA	MYANMAR	THAILAND
JAPAN	NORTH KOREA	VIETNAM

Find your way through the maze.

HIGHLIGHT

ROAD TRIP!

The favorite snack of road trip travelers is nuts.

•

The cost of the first road trip from New York to California in 1903 was $8,000.

•

The highest speed limit in the US is 85 mph in Texas between Austin and San Antonio.

•

The two most popular end points on a road trip are Yellowstone National Park and Disneyworld.

•

During the holidays, over 93 million people drive to visit their family.

•

The most popular road trip games are I Spy, the License Plate Game, and 20 Questions.

•

The most common street name in the US is Second Street.

Use the code below to read the secret message.

◎	⅄	☼	□	🌢	✓	❖	♦	✿	✞	☺	✎	♒
A	B	C	D	E	F	G	H	I	J	K	L	M

★	↑	↓	●	⌘	☸	✖	⁂	▣	✹	✂	※	❄
N	O	P	Q	R	S	T	U	V	W	X	Y	Z

✹ ♦ 🌢 ★   ※ ↑ ⁂   ✖ ◎ ✎ ☺ ,

※ ↑ ⁂   ☸ ♦ ↑ ⁂ ✎ □   ◎ ✎ ✹ ◎ ※ ☸

⅄ 🌢   ☺ ✿ ★ □   ◎ ★ □   ✹ ✿ ☸ 🌢 .

✖ ♦ 🌢 ★   ※ ↑ ⁂   ✹ ✿ ✎ ✎   ⅄ 🌢

◎ ⅄ ✎ 🌢   ✖ ↑   ◎ ★ ☸ ✹ 🌢 ⌘

🌢 ▣ 🌢 ⌘ ※ ↑ ★ 🌢   ✿ ★   ✖ ♦ 🌢

✹ ◎ ※   ※ ↑ ⁂   ☸ ♦ ↑ ⁂ ✎ □ .

Answer on page 127

Draw a line from the beginning to the end that passes through each box with a car in it once. The line can go up, down, left, or right, but cannot go diagonal.

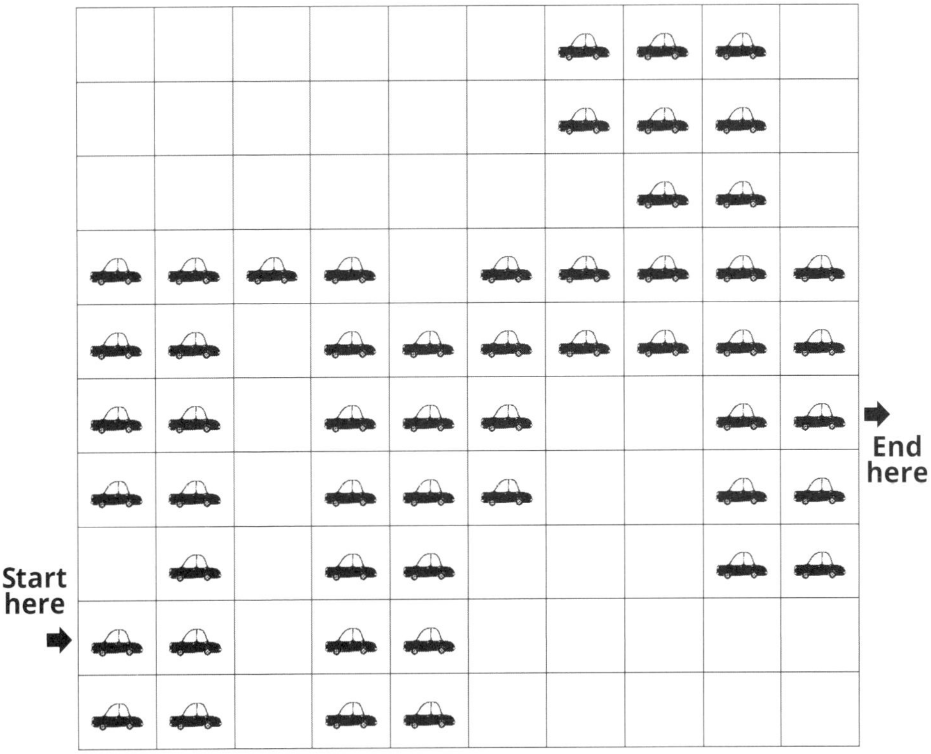

Spot the ten Differences Between the two Pictures.

On a scale of 1 to 10 how easy do you find it to extend grace to others?

______

Why do you think that is?

COURAGE

Be strong in the Lord and in his mighty power. Put on the full armor of God, so that you can take your stand against the devil's schemes.

EPHESIANS 6:10-11 NIV

Imagine you are fighting a battle with all your might. The swords are flying, and the enemies are falling. All of a sudden you see a fearless leader at the front slaying dragons right and left. Anyone who dares attack him loses badly because he has so much skill and power.

Jesus is the leader in our battles. He fights with us and for us. He fills us with his strength and courage to face everything that comes our way. Nothing can crush us, and nothing can defeat us because he is so strong.

When you are facing something difficult, look to the leader of the battle and let him fight for you!

Unscramble the words to read the secret message.

E B   N T R O G S   D N A
_ _   _ _ _ _ _ _   _ _ _

R S O G E U C O U A
_ _ _ _ _ _ _ _ _ _ !

O D   O T N   E B
_ _   _ _ _   _ _

A D I R A F   R O
_ _ _ _ _ _   _ _

G R D U S I E D C O A
_ _ _ _ _ _ _ _ _ _ _ .

R O F   H E T   R D L O
_ _ _   _ _ _   _ _ _ _

R U O Y   O G D   S I
_ _ _ _   _ _ _   _ _

T H W I   U O Y
_ _ _ _   _ _ _

H E V E R W E R   O Y U   O G
_ _ _ _ _ _ _ _   _ _ _   _ _ .

Answer on page 127

N

N A X

R I D Y B

T A G D C U L

A D C E V B J A I

N X Z S R X E Y Y B B

Z L E H A I R N S B V T E

A W O L A G A E L J I G L Y R

N D D D N C A K C M I L U R P P I

I E G Y P T I D G H A N A W L I W E A

A O E L J Z V R A P U B J A B W W T Q F A

P G U O F W T M D P G N F C E H S D I

C N W A A A T H A D A R Z I A U B

P O Q J H K O A T V N O M E I

I C C T N X I I G P D A M

H E U O A L R I F U A

E O A F A A H S N

S Y V M H X G

Y N O Y I

K S J

W

Find the African countries in the word search below.

CONGO	LIBERIA	RWANDA
EGYPT	LIBYA	SOMALIA
ETHIOPIA	MADAGASCAR	SOUTH AFRICA
GHANA	NAMIBIA	TANZANIA
KENYA	NIGERIA	UGANDA

Find your way to the center of the maze.

HIGHLIGHT

SKI TRIP!

Skiing and snowboarding vacations are most popular among people ages 16-24.

•

The word "ski" comes from a Norwegian word that means a split piece of wood.

•

The first downhill skiing race was in 1879. It took place in Sweden.

•

Skiing is one of the fastest non-motorized sports on land. Professional speed skiers have been clocked traveling 150 mph.

•

The first snowboard was called a "snurfer." A man built a special surfboard to ride on the snow.

•

The longest recorded time spent skiing is 202 hours and 1 minute.

•

"Skiing" is the only word in the English language that has a double "i" exactly in the middle of the word.

Circle the skier who came first in the Downhill ski race.

Answer on page 127

I LOVE
TRAVEL

Dear God, you commanded me to always have courage. With you, I don't need to be afraid even when I am not in familiar places. Thank you for being with me wherever I go.

Draw a line from the beginning to the end that passes through each box with a mountain in it once. The line can go up, down, left, or right, but cannot go diagonal.

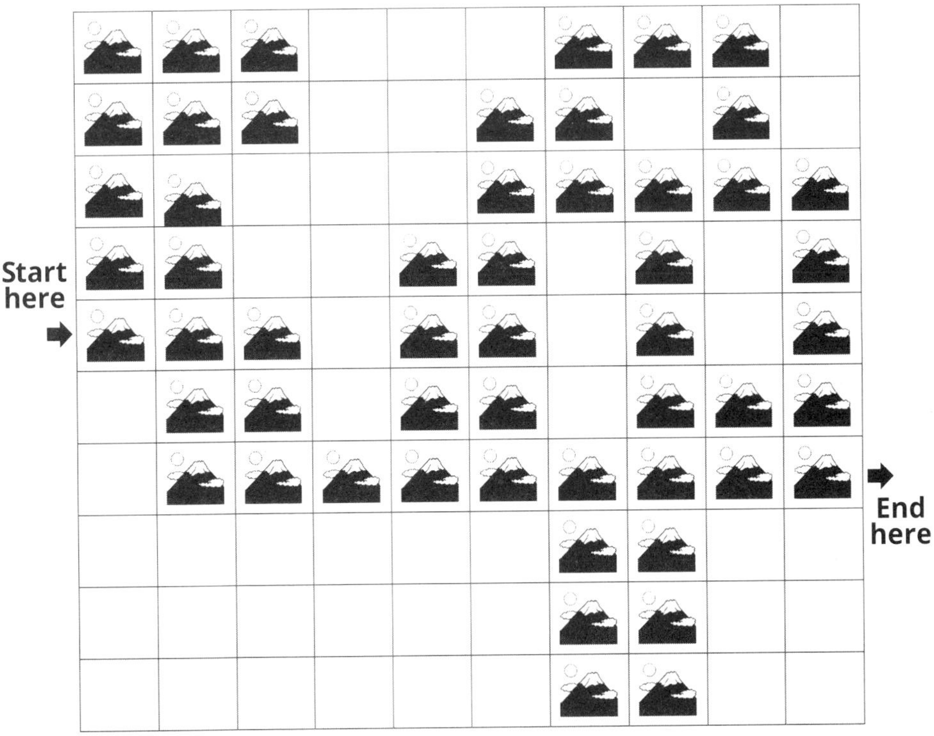

Draw a line from the images at the bottom of the page to their shadow buddies above.

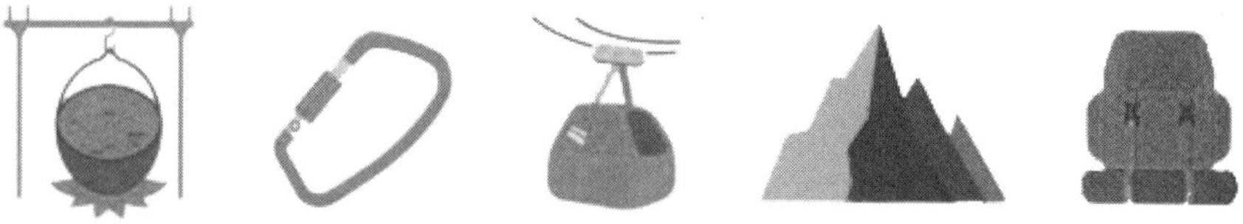

Answer on page 128

Word of the Day:

COURAGE!

Write your definition of the word courage below, and then write an example of how you have been courageous lately.

PRAISE

Enter his gates with thanksgiving
and his courts with praise;
give thanks to him and praise his name.

Psalm 100:4 NIV

Before you travel, things might seem a little busy. You are trying to finish up all those last chores or tasks, and you still have to pack! It's important to do all the things on your list, but don't forget the most important thing of all—praise!

God wants you to remember him and thank him. It helps to be thankful to God throughout your day. Stopping to praise him gives you peace and joy that can last the whole day, and it can help you stay focused on the tasks you are trying to complete.

God cares about you and your vacation. Bring him in to your travel plans and thank him for the wonderful things you get to experience each day you are away.

Dear God, you deserve so much more praise than I can give. Even the sun and moon cannot praise you enough. Thank you for all the blessings you have given me and for sending your Son to die for me.

Replacing one letter at a time, change THANK to PEACE!

THANK

_ _ _ _ _ ponder

_ _ _ _ _ old English way of saying yours

_ _ _ _ _ glow, glisten, sparkle

_ _ _ _ _ backbone

_ _ _ _ _ desire to harm

_ _ _ _ _ ejects saliva

_ _ _ _ _ cuts apart

_ _ _ _ _ narrow strips of wood

_ _ _ _ _ fine-grained rock

_ _ _ _ _ used to serve food

_ _ _ _ _ location

PEACE

Answer on page 128

E N A L P R I A T
H C M P M K I A P A
S P T N O A E I Y
T S R A B T J K
I U M T O B O P
B Q A V B N R T
F H X Y U L O C L
T I R R X I O Y
R C S R I A L C
A O O E K S L L
C E C F S S A E
T R W S T L B D
O C O U E J R U
R H R B J Y I Z G
Z Z W N I A R T
K Y A C H T Z V
A Y R X O B C B
Y L A H K C U R T
U C A B O X Q Q A Z
B I C Y C L E J D

Find the different ways you can travel in the word search above.

AIRPLANE	HOT AIR BALLOON	TAXI
BICYCLE	JETSKI	TRACTOR
BUS	MOTORCYCLE	TRAIN
CAR	SAILBOAT	TRUCK
FERRY	SUBWAY	YACHT

Using the message below, break the code and figure out which letter corresponds to which number.

	21			2			3		24			6
A	B	C	D	E	F	G	H	I	J	K	L	M
			25	4						17		18
N	O	P	Q	R	S	T	U	V	W	X	Y	Z

7 4 5 16 8 2   1 3 2   13 20 4 19

22 4 20 6   1 3 2   8 26 16 2 8.

7 4 5 16 8 2   3 16 6   3 16 12 3

5 21 20 23 2   1 3 2   2 5 4 1 3.

7 4 5 16 8 2   3 16 6,   8 15 11

5 11 19   6 20 20 11.   7 4 5 16 8 2

3 16 6,   5 13 13   9 20 15

8 3 16 11 16 11 12   8 1 5 4 8.   13 2 1

1 3 2 6   7 4 5 16 8 2   1 3 2

13 20 4 19   21 2 10 5 15 8 2   1 3 2 9

14 2 4 2   10 4 2 5 1 2 19   21 9

3 16 8   10 20 6 6 5 11 19.

Answer on page 128

Find your way through the maze.

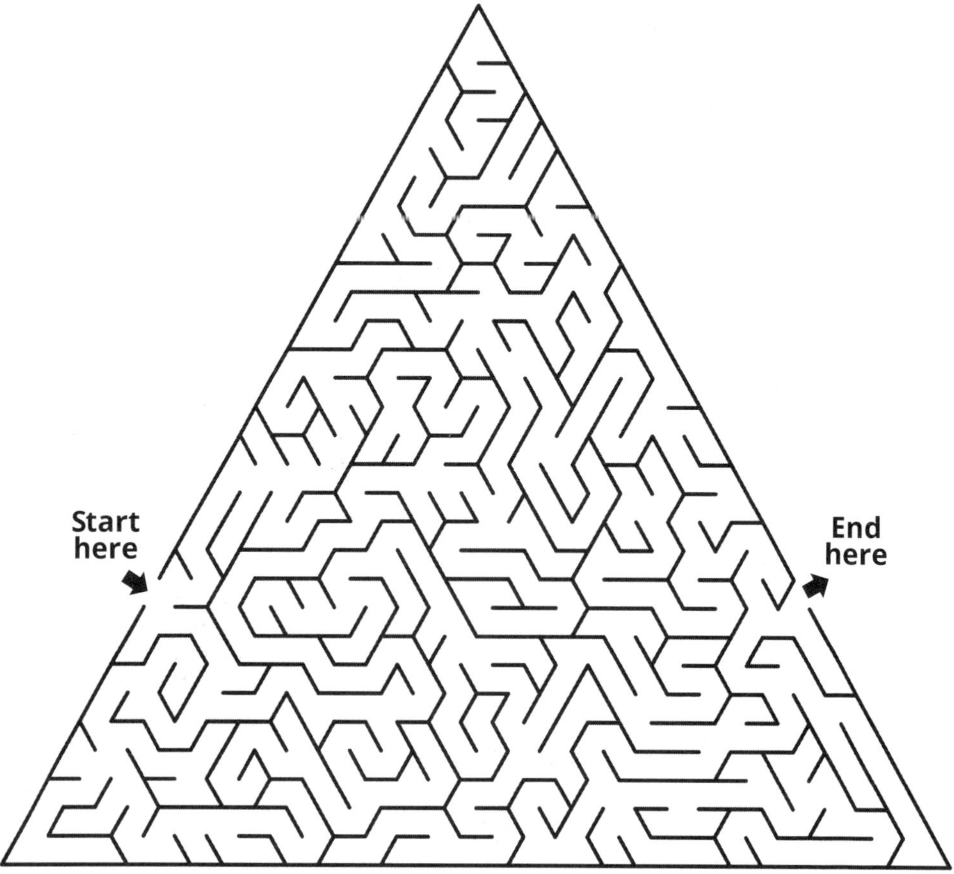

Use the Pictures Below to figure out the secret message.

  2

________ a new ________ ________

 – C + L 

the ____________. ____________ his praise

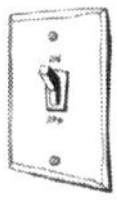 

everywhere ________ the ____________.

Praise him, ________ people who ________

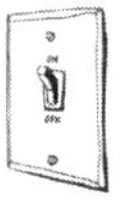   

________ the ________ and ________ ____________

 – H + L  – F

who ____________ ________ them.

Answer on page 128

Spot the ten Differences Between the two Pictures.

HIGHLIGHT
SAFARI!

A lion's roar can be heard up to five miles away. It is one of the loudest noises made by an animal.

•

A baby giraffe can weigh up to 220 pounds when it is born.

•

Ostriches are the fastest two-legged animals. They can reach speeds of up to 60 mph.

•

Chances are, if you see a lion on a safari, it will be sleeping. Lions sleep about 20 hours per day.

•

Elephant babies often suck their trunks for comfort.

•

About 4.5 million people visit Africa to see safari lands each year.

•

The four favorite African safari locations are Botswana, Kenya, Tanzania, and Zambia.

•

Africa's "big five" are the five most talked about animals in Africa. They are lions, elephants, rhinos, buffalo, and leopards.

•

Neither black nor white rhinos have front teeth which means they have to use their lips to eat.

Using the word

PRAISE,

list the ways you can thank God for his many Blessings!

P

R

A

I

S

E

ANSWERS

Pg. 5
Jesus Christ is the same yesterday and today and forever.
Hebrews 13:8 NIRV

Pg. 6
ROCK, RACK, RACE, RICE, RIPE, ROPE, HOPE

Pg. 7
We have this hope as an anchor for the soul, firm and secure.
Hebrews 6:19 NIV

Pg. 10
Brush, toothpaste, tennis shoes, sunscreen

Pg. 15

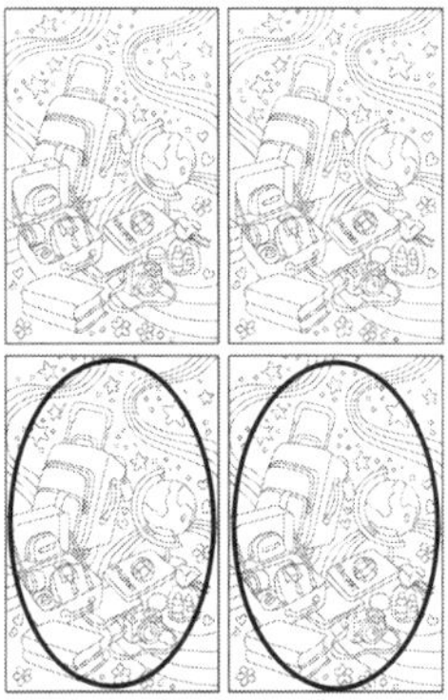

Pg. 17

3	12	8	14	2	21	11	16	4	26	25	19	20
A	**B**	**C**	**D**	**E**	**F**	**G**	**H**	**I**	**J**	**K**	**L**	**M**
9	15	7	24	6	1	5	17	13	10	23	18	22
N	**O**	**P**	**Q**	**R**	**S**	**T**	**U**	**V**	**W**	**X**	**Y**	**Z**

Wise people can also listen and learn;
even they can find good advice in these words.
Proverbs 1:5 NCV

Pg. 22
We can make our plans,
but the LORD determines our steps.
Proverbs 16:9 NLT

Pg. 26
WHINE, WHILE, WHALE, SHALE, SHAKE, SHANE, SHANK, THANK

Pg. 27
Across: 2. Journey. 5. Vacation. 7. Tour guide. 9. Suitcase. 10. Ticket. 11. Treasure. 12. Explore.
Down: 1. Lost. 3. Farewell. 4. Map. 6. Insurance. 8. Culture.

Pg. 29
Rejoice always, pray continually, give thanks in all circumstances.
1 Thessalonians 5:16–18 NIV

Pg. 31

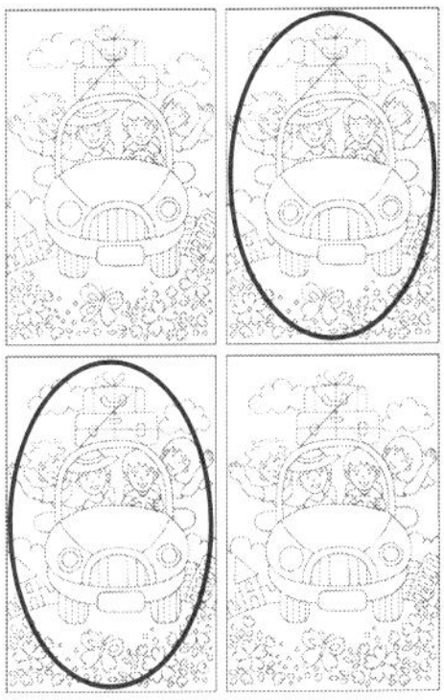

Pg. 37
There is a time to tear apart and a time to sew together.
There is a time to be silent and a time to speak.
Ecclesiastes 3:7 NCV

Pg. 40
Those who are careful about what they say keep themselves out of trouble.
Proverbs 21:23 NIRV

Pg. 45
POTTER, CREPT, OCTET, OTTER, TORTE, COPE, CORE, CROP, POET, PORE, PORT, ROPE, ROTE, TORE, TOTE, COP, COT, ORE, PET, POT

Pg. 56
Don't do anything only to get ahead. Don't do it because you are proud. Instead, be humble. Value others more than yourselves.
Philippians 2:3 NIRV

Pg. 57

Andre went to Australasia; Rita went to Africa; Kevin went to Asia; Mollie went to South America; Tiana went to North America.

Pg. 60

Show respect for all people: Love the brothers and sisters of God's family, respect God, honor the king.
1 Peter 2:17 NCV

Pg. 65

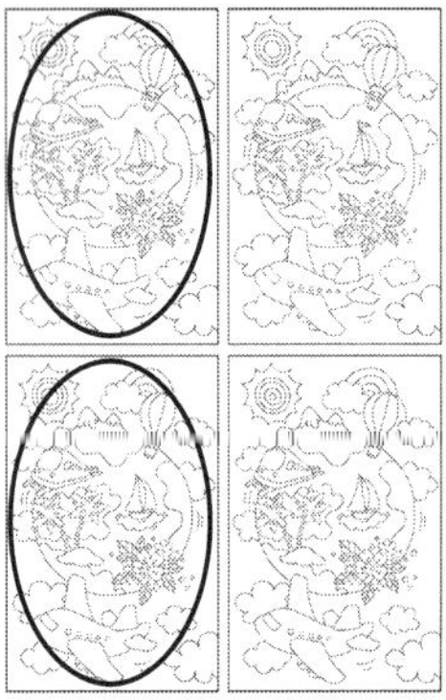

Pg. 66

Ann babysat; Lizzie cleaned; Miguel cooked a meal; Jamaal walked the dog; Jasmine mowed the lawn.

Pg. 67

Across: 3. Canyon. 7. Mountain. 8. Island. 10. River. 11. Beach.
Down: 1. Valley. 2. Volcano. 4. Plain. 5. Ocean. 6. Glacier. 9. Lake. 10. Reef.

Pg. 69

Share with the Lord's people who are in need. Welcome others into your homes.
Romans 12:13 ICB

Pg. 75

Austria, Belgium, France, Germany, Netherlands, Switzerland, Bulgaria, Hungary, Poland, Romania, Russia, Ukraine

Pg. 76
Always be joyful because you belong to the Lord. I will say it again. Be joyful!
Philippians 4:4 NIRV

Pg. 80
You always show me the path of life.
You will fill me with joy when I am with you.
Psalm 16:11 NIRV

Pg. 86
Be sure that no one pays back wrong for wrong. But always try to do what is good for each other and for all people.
1 Thessalonians 5:15 ICB

Pg. 87
Ann – ní hăo – Mandarin
Jamaal – hola – Spanish
Lizzie – namaste - Hindi
Miguel – ciao – Italian
Jasmine – bonjour – French

Pg. 91
Remember to welcome strangers, because some who have done this have welcomed angels without knowing it.
Hebrews 13:2 NCV

Pg. 95
MEAN, BEAN, BEAD, BEND, BIND, KIND

Pg. 99
When you talk, you should always be kind and wise. Then you will be able to answer everyone in the way you should.
Colossians 4:6 ICB

Pg. 105
"Be strong and courageous! Do not be afraid or discouraged. For the LORD your God is with you wherever you go."
Joshua 1:9 NLT

Pg. 109
The skier on the right (with black hair).

Pg. 112

Pg. 115

THANK, THINK, THINE, SHINE, SPINE, SPITE, SPITS, SLITS, SLATS, SLATE, PLATE, PLACE, PEACE

Pg. 117

5	21	10	19	2	22	12	3	16	24	26	13	6
A	**B**	**C**	**D**	**E**	**F**	**G**	**H**	**I**	**J**	**K**	**L**	**M**
11	20	7	25	4	8	1	15	23	14	17	9	18
N	**O**	**P**	**Q**	**R**	**S**	**T**	**U**	**V**	**W**	**X**	**Y**	**Z**

Praise the LORD from the skies. Praise him high above the earth.
Praise him, sun and moon. Praise him, all you shining stars.
Let them praise the LORD, because they were created by his command.
Psalm 148:1-5 NCV

Pg. 119

Sing a new song to the Lord. Sing his praise everywhere on the earth.
Praise him, you people who sail on the seas and you animals who live in them.
Isaiah 42:10 ICB